The FAITH

———

that transcends HUMANITY

Ishaq Mir

BLUEROSE PUBLISHERS
India | U.K.

Copyright © Ishaq Mir 2024

All rights reserved by author. No part of this publication may be reproduced, stored in a retrieval system or transmitted in any form or by any means, electronic, mechanical, photocopying, recording or otherwise, without the prior permission of the author. Although every precaution has been taken to verify the accuracy of the information contained herein, the publisher assumes no responsibility for any errors or omissions. No liability is assumed for damages that may result from the use of information contained within.

BlueRose Publishers takes no responsibility for any damages, losses, or liabilities that may arise from the use or misuse of the information, products, or services provided in this publication.

For permissions requests or inquiries regarding this publication,
please contact:

BLUEROSE PUBLISHERS
www.BlueRoseONE.com
info@bluerosepublishers.com
+91 8882 898 898
+4407342408967

ISBN: 978-93-5989-247-4

Cover design: Muskan Sachdeva
Typesetting: Pooja Sharma

First Edition: January 2024

Review

As seen in the extract, Ishaaq Mir's literary style is a brilliant combination of emotional depth, intellectual thought, and a heartfelt appeal to universal human ideals. The story begins with a touching tribute to Mir's late father, a carrier of human brotherhood whose nightly prayers included everyone without exception. This establishes a personal connection between the author and the reader by setting a respectful and genuinely emotional tone. Mir provides significant philosophical views on the nature of mankind, highlighting the safeguarding of human values. The discussion dives into the ramifications of sacrificing these ideals, providing a bleak image of a society ripe for disaster as a result of the predominance of hatred and mistrust.

The text is distinguished by an appeal to universal values, forcefully fighting for all people's connections. Mir opposes anger and arrogance as threats to civilised society, portraying them as hideous stains on humanity's forehead. This plea instills a sense of shared responsibility in readers by urging them to consider the larger ramifications of their actions. The "fire of hatred" and the "stain on the forehead," for example, enhance the story by making abstract notions physical and compelling.

Mir's writing style shines in its simplicity and accessibility. Despite acknowledging that he is not a professional writer, this admission adds authenticity and humility to his words. The straightforward language ensures that the message reaches a wide audience without unnecessary complexity. Mir's sincerity is palpable as he shares his personal reflections and the supernatural encouragement that drove him to use the pen as a medium to awaken humanity from the deep slumber of hatred and arrogance.

The narrative takes on a global perspective, addressing the increasing trend of hatred worldwide. Mir calls attention to the dangers of allowing any form of hateful thought to permeate society. The writing serves as a call to action, urging readers to reflect on their actions and choices. Beyond merely avoiding hatred, Mir actively promotes compassion and understanding, asking readers to ponder the profound message he conveys.

This geographical reference adds a layer of cultural richness, providing insight into the author's surroundings and experiences. While Mir's perspective is deeply rooted in his cultural context, the universal themes he addresses make his writing resonate beyond regional boundaries.

In essence, Ishaaq Mir's writing is a powerful and authentic expression of a deep concern for humanity. The narrative is a testament to the transformative power of humility, compassion, and understanding. Mir's writing style captures the complexity of human emotions and societal challenges, weaving them into a narrative that transcends cultural boundaries. As readers, we are invited not only to witness Mir's reflections but also to actively engage in the collective responsibility of preserving the core principles that make us human.

"The Faith That Transcends: Humanity"

"The purpose of human life is to serve, and to show compassion and the will to help others."

— *Albert Schweitzer.*

Attribution

In the name of my respected late father, who was the bearer of human brotherhood; it was his routine to cry and pray during nights for the entire mankind without discrimination. The adherents of all creeds and caste were equal to him and he considered them all as members of one family (humanity). He considered humanity to be the greatest bond among them and emphasized increasing harmony through it. He was against all kinds of hatred and considered any person having such thoughts as an ugly stain on the forehead of civilized society.

May he rest in eternal peace!

Introduction

Humanity makes us the greatest of all the creatures. Human values are the guarantee of protection for all. It is through this virtue that a strong and sincere relationship between human beings and other creatures is established. Today, human beings are compromising with this original identity. The result is that we are inviting terrible destruction and devastation. It is only because of this 'compromise' that hatred and mistrust have taken deep roots in our societies. We are all busy competing with each other which has made us obsessed and selfish. We always remain ready to dig pits for others without thinking that we are going to fall. The fire of hatred we have set, perhaps to demean others is surely going to perish us all.

People from every sect and class will have to bear the fire they set because nobody can isolate him or herself from the world we all live in. Since hatred and arrogance are other names for insanity, therefore, everybody among us who holds the same stubbornness will get drowned in it.

Today, when the trend of hatred is increasing almost all over the world, there is no shortage of equipment to wreak havoc and destruction as well. In such a situation, we are fanning the fire by allowing any kind of hateful thought to reach us. By doing this, we are directly ignoring the dangers and the consequences of which surely be borne by everyone. When a volcano erupts, it sweeps away everything in its path no matter how strong.

Taking humanity lightly, going against its basic principles, and transgressing its prescribed limits, how can one save himself from the dangers against which humanity defends like a shield? And by ignoring the importance of this shield, we are making a big mistake. We are raising a big question mark on the security of the world we live in. Therefore, to promote any kind of hatred and arrogance is like to act as a spark on the pile of gunpowder and to invite countless troubles for humanity as a whole. Be assured, this will only kill humanity and create distances among human beings in different names.

Today's world is already struggling with big problems. Without research, large numbers of people are spreading, what they hear, without using their intellect. Unfortunately, highly educated and capable people are involved in this menace which has resulted in spreading hatred like wildfire. Hence, the people who were meant to benefit humanity are otherwise cutting its roots and making it hollow. When people with positive and creative intellect also go against the basic principles of humanity, it means that the whole world is in danger. It also means that our societies will automatically lose the high qualities of mercy and compassion, and our hearts are bound to turn into stones.

Human beings can go to any extent then. They will feel the pleasure of music in other's screams after hurting them.

Now think that by doing this are not we going out of the circle of humanity, are we not becoming enemies of our own lives and the world we live in? Remember, hatred and arrogance make us barbarians and these inhuman values alienate us from humanity. God forbid if it happens, it will not take long for the world to turn into a sea of pain. Then there will be no one to listen to anyone's cries because everyone will be going through a similar situation.

Therefore, by increasing any kind of hatred, we are doing a great injustice to ourselves by directly attacking humanity and hurting it deeply. We have no idea, that by doing so, we are opening the doors of all kinds of troubles for the whole humankind.

This booklet of mine is a humble attempt to wake the humanity among human beings. Since I am not a professional writer, there is every possibility that my attempt will be full of loopholes. But, believe me, this booklet is a result of some supernatural power that encouraged me to use the pen as a medium to try to awaken humanity from a deep slumber, the slumber of hatred, arrogance, exclusivity, etc.

I feel satisfied and hope that my endeavor will be taken positively by the esteemed readers. At the same time, it is my humble request to the valued readers not to give heed to my mistakes but please ponder on the message I want to convey.

Thanks

Ishaaq Mir (Srinagar, Kashmir, India)

Contents

Humanity 1
Hatred 6
Hatred victimizes innocents 8
Collective threat 11
Anxieties 16
Nature 22
Deceptions 29
Divisions 32
The beginning of change 35
Introspection 38
Acknowledgments 43
Love 46
Leadership 49
The spirit of service 55
Selfishness 58
Things to do 60
Be positive 66
Conclusion 73

Humanity

Humanism refers to the collective characteristics, behaviors, and attributes of human beings as a whole. It encompasses the essence of being human, including our, intellectual, emotional, ethical, and, social dimensions. Humanity is often associated with the qualities and values that define our species, such as compassion, empathy, reason, creativity, and the capacity for moral judgment.

Humanism is a philosophical and ethical perspective that emphasizes human values, dignity, and well-being. It is a belief system or worldview that affirms the worth and agencies of human beings valuing their capacity to reason, think critically, and make moral choices.

Humanity emphasizes the importance of human interests, concerns, and potential. Humanity values reason, sympathy, evidence, and of course, science as reliable methods for understanding the world and addressing human problems.

Humanity also emphasizes the idea that humans have inherent rights and should be treated with respect and compassion. It recognizes the value of individual freedom, respect, autonomy, and equality. Humanists advocate for social justice, equality, respect, human rights, and the well-being of all individuals.

When we talk about "humanity," we are referring to the collective human race or the condition of being human. It encompasses the qualities, characteristics, and experiences that are unique to humans. Humanity is often used to describe acts of compassion, kindness, and empathy towards others.

Humanity can also refer to the broader human community and the shared responsibility we have towards one another. It highlights the importance of recognizing and respecting the dignity and worth of all individuals, regardless of their differences. Humanistic principles often align with the idea of promoting the well-being and flourishing of humanity as a whole.

Humanity is a philosophical perspective that emphasizes human values, reason, and well-being. It recognizes the worth and agency of individuals and promotes ethical behavior and social justice. Humanity, on the other hand, refers to the collective human race and encompasses qualities such as concern, understanding, and shared responsibility towards others.

Observing the daily occurrences and events happening around the world, a clear picture emerges that humanity and human values are gradually diminishing. The reason behind this is the increasing divisions and walls of hatred between individuals and different factions, which are growing rapidly. As each passing day goes by, its circle expands. The result is that innocent people become an easy target amidst this hatred, and they continue to suffer and endure various forms of oppression and violence.

Now, cruelty and injustice are being observed to such an extent that it seems that this is the foundation of the new world. And to everybody's surprise, it is being done by those who claim to belong to an advanced era of progress. They are building bridges of praise for themselves, highlighting the achievements of this century, and creating their identity as individuals who are well-read, knowledgeable, and possessors of new ideas.

They always claim to believe in practical actions, being advocates of humanity, far-sighted individuals with great qualities, and making grand claims. They even proclaim technology to be the great feat of human intelligence, declaring it as the revolutionary power that has eliminated distances among people around the world, bringing them so close that the world has become a global village for everyone.

When we examine the facts on the ground, it unveils a different story. Unfortunately, a large number of people in this 'new time' and 'advanced era' are clouded by arrogance and pride, nurturing an internal prejudice and narrow-mindedness. They are poisoning the beautiful and enchanting cosmos of nature with their hateful thoughts.

Furthermore, they belittle and undermine those individuals who, with their intellect and hard work, have played a crucial role in the progress of the world, elevating it to great heights. They have revolutionized almost all fields associated with human life and, through their astonishing achievements, have elevated human dignity, instilling a sense of pride in everyone. This is the fruit of their endeavors, a testament to the progress achieved in the twenty-first century. It would not be wrong to say that all these individuals, without any discrimination, are carrying humanity in their minds while pursuing their work.

A significant number of people, encompassing individuals from diverse backgrounds and social classes, have embraced within themselves various forms of hateful thoughts. Their actions have brought shame and disgrace upon humanity. It seems as though they have taken upon themselves the monumental task of eradicating it from the world. Consequently, incidents of hatred have become prevalent worldwide, causing deep anguish to those who hold empathy and compassion in their hearts. These disturbing occurrences instill a profound fear, as one cannot be certain that they won't fall victim to this hatred.

Situations are created in such a way that at any time, in any place, and the mind of anyone, certain negative thoughts will awaken. Then it won't take long for them to turn into wild beasts, crushing and destroying all human values, making themselves an easy target for busy and absorbed people in their world, and unleashing wrath.

Claiming to herald a new era and a new age is a big deception. We have 'progressed' so much that being human has become a great crime. Without any fault or mistake, one is being made guilty and then the punishment is also self-imposed. This is the reality of the 'advanced' age in which we are 'progressing' like the Stone Age in terms of thinking.

Hatred

Contrary to humanity, hatred is an intense and deep-seated negative emotion or feeling of extreme animosity, hostility, or aversion towards someone or something. It typically involves a strong sense of anger, resentment, or disgust, often accompanied by a desire for harm, destruction, or exclusion. Hatred can stem from various sources, such as personal experiences, differences in beliefs, ideologies, cultures, or even prejudices based on race, religion, gender, or other factors. It is characterized by an active and enduring dislike, often leading to a desire to devalue, demean, or harm the target of one's hatred. Hatred can have significant social, psychological, and emotional consequences for both individuals and communities.

Hatred is against the principles of humanity. It goes against the values of compassion, empathy, understanding, and respect for others that are essential to fostering a harmonious and inclusive society. Hatred can lead to division, conflict, and suffering, as it often fuels discrimination, violence, and oppression. Recognizing and combating hatred is important for promoting peace, justice, and equality among all individuals, regardless of their differences. Embracing love, acceptance, and tolerance can help build a more compassionate and humane world.

Hatred victimizes innocents

Today, so many innocent people, in the guise of hatred, are being pushed into big calamities, where this hatred has become a blinding pain for their lives and the places they belong to. They crush their dreams and aspirations, and create darkness upon darkness, leading them into ruins. Suddenly, upon those innocent people who were happily living their lives, showers of sorrow pour down, throwing them into the ocean of pain. And then, they are forced to make pain their companion, stealing their joys and creating a habit of living with sorrow.

Countless innocent people in the world are being oppressed and persecuted in the name of different ideologies, beliefs, races, and religions. The level of injustice and tyranny they face is extreme. It reaches a point where these individuals are not even allowed to interact with others. However, some hypocritically hold onto hateful thoughts, considering them acceptable for themselves, without seeing any wrongdoing in their actions. This mentality is growing day by day.

We are witnessing a significant shift in people's thoughts and attitudes. Many individuals who possess a good intellect, consciousness, higher education, and skills are falling prey to this mindset of hatred. They are losing all their virtues and abilities in favor of embracing this inhumane ideology. This poses a significant threat to humanity, creating a new danger that needs to be eliminated from the world. Their actions continue to be painful as they do not feel any remorse for their inhumane acts. They consider them a means to satisfy their hearts and strive to find new ways to assert their dominance over others.

The freedom of expression, facilitated by technology and social media, makes it easier for them to fulfill their agendas. They utilize any means possible, including speech and writing, to surpass the boundaries of humanity. Even good people, in some way or another, become victims of crossing the designated limits of humanity themselves. This, in turn, exposes innocent individuals to the risk of calamities, as the door for misfortune opens upon them through a single wrong statement or a malicious rumor. Consequently, they become a dreadful affliction for countless blameless individuals, leading to the destruction of their lives and the places where they reside.

How many people continue to perform acts of inhumanity throughout the day? It includes individuals of almost all beliefs, colors, races, and backgrounds. Are they performing these actions to suppress their guilt? Or are they doing it to show empathy for specific groups of people? Many see it as a convenient means to make themselves famous. They perceive it as the best way to achieve their interests. However, what about those innocent people who, become a target of danger without any fault or wrongdoing on their part? It would not take long for them to bear the burden of hatred projected upon them.

Collective threat

In this current era, known as the era of progress, unfortunately, anyone living in one corner of the world can pose a danger to those living in another corner who may not even know about it. Nor will they necessarily agree with their thoughts and beliefs. Nevertheless, because the hateful people have all the necessary resources, they can use their malicious minds to disturb any peaceful environment and create a threat to their safety. By creating collisions among those who live their lives with peace and tranquility, it can turn them against each other and create animosity and division. To the extent that they may even be willing to confront each other face to face, either to kill or to be killed. No consideration will be given to children, women, and the elderly.

Originally, the idea was that everyone, regardless of their enthusiasm, should not let their passion overshadow their senses and should support humanity wholeheartedly, without inflicting any harm.

We are all humans first. After that, we can be something else. Therefore, how can we cause pain and suffering by hatred to innocent human beings and leave them in agony? Our belief does not permit it. Humans were created for the sake of compassion, love, and friendship, igniting the flame of humanity in everyone so that all of God's creation can benefit from it.

Unfortunately, today it is rare to see things and thoughts like humanity, which is the greatest bond between us. It is the best means for connecting and maintaining harmony with each other. We are losing its importance by creating distances.

Today, even though we are educated, knowledgeable, and have a higher consciousness, we do not use our intellect correctly. We become ignorant even after knowing and understanding everything. We immediately spread any statement we hear without verifying it. The recipients also accept that information with such seriousness, as if they had personally witnessed such happening. However in comparison to one's existence, every action should be scrutinized and thoroughly investigated before concluding right or wrong. But, we do not consider it necessary. Thus, saying "no" to those who say "no" without knowledge or research and "yes" to those who say "yes," has become the order of the day.

For this reason, it is not a problem for it to become illiterate despite being educated. Circumstances and situations have made it easier for humans today to be misled. Negative thinking has engulfed humanity to such an extent that impossible things seem true. If someone says that a curtain has been drawn over the sun to deprive a certain class of people of its light, and barriers have been created in the air for some living in specific areas, will not only be accepted but also spread like anything.

The world seems ready to believe in many impossible things and continue to propagate them. Although everyone knows that no matter how much effort is made, one cannot achieve everything. Yet, what can be expected from the so-called great human intelligence?

Day by day, humans are losing their ability to understand and comprehend, and instead, they are relying solely on their misleading ambitions. The biggest reason for this is the rise of hateful thinking. Today, all around the world, we see highly educated individuals with brilliant minds, who have excelled in various fields, surrendering their abilities by embracing negative thoughts, prejudice, and arrogance. If they were to use their intellectual capabilities with positive thinking, how much could they contribute to humanity? Alongside this, they could achieve greatness by raising the banner of love. They would become cherished in the world and receive the most precious thing, which brings peace and tranquility to the heart.

If someone believes that hateful thinking provides solace to their heart and considers it a noble deed for themselves, it is a great deception of Satan or the devil. It is a trap that engulfs their hearts and minds. This allows it to manipulate them and turn their minds into instruments of hatred towards their fellow human beings. It becomes so intense and irrational that they start attacking innocent people in various ways, causing them suffering, distress, and hardship, ultimately turning their lives into a living hell. As a result, humanity is left apologetic, and a sinister stain is cast upon it. Observing the heartless and merciless behavior towards their human brethren, even mute animals will be deeply affected and take pride in their existence as beings devoid of empathy and compassion.

The observation is correct that hateful thinking hurts human nature and it diminishes our abilities and capabilities. It leads to conflicts and violence among ourselves hindering human progress.

All those who regardless of their differences or social classes, live anywhere in the world, those who have built a cave within themselves for hatred and made it their flying banner, who are adamant about inflicting the punishment of hatred on innocent people under different names, and who have become addicted to plunging others into pain and suffering. Those who do not feel any shame or remorse for their deeds and words cannot escape from it.

They have detached the bonds of humanity from their souls. That is why hatred has made them so deaf and blind. They take pleasure in the cries and screams of those who suffer due to their actions and consider it as a tool to soothe their hearts.

They have created a world for themselves and their loved ones, adorned with grand dreams, only to witness tears of blood streaming from other's eyes. It fascinates them because such people are habitual in taking pleasure out of toxic sounds. Such people see treasures of happiness and contentment in immersing someone in the quagmire of difficulties and tribulations, and they perceive the opportunity to celebrate by trapping someone in the whirlpool of worries as their victory.

Worries and mental burdens have trapped everyone in the grip. The reason for this is that we are all living in an era of so-called competition and superficiality, where every relationship and connection is measured only in terms of money. The brotherhood, compassion, mutual support, coming together in times of joy and sorrow, human friendship, and noble intentions for everyone—all of these have now become old tales.

Therefore, today's individuals have entered the battlefield of life, fighting alone in a lonely field. They are exerting all their strength and energy without pausing for a moment, ignoring the variations of hot and cold, rain and snow, day and night.

Anxieties

Anxiety is a normal human emotion characterized by feelings of unease, worry, fear, or apprehension about future events, situations, or uncertainties. It is a natural stress response and can be experienced by anyone from time to time. However, when anxiety becomes excessive, persistent, and starts interfering with daily life, it may be classified as an anxiety disorder.

Many of us try to take advantage of every opportunity, until they reach their destination in the journey of life, shedding their sweat and blood. They endure every oppression of the times without complaint and even manage to smile in any situation, which is a characteristic that helps them conceal their sorrows.

Countless necessities have become solid walls, creating a large puzzle in hearts and minds with every new morning, bringing forth new challenges.

Restlessness and despair, consumed internally, make every person suffer greatly, despite appearing carefree and optimistic from the outside. In reality, they are burning from within, while their world burns outside. If only there was a device invented that could measure someone's pain and suffering, an investigation using that device, everyone would be astonished to discover how someone manages to stay alive after reaching an extreme level of suffering.

See around yourself, today's humans have become exhausted and worn out in the struggle of life and the blows of circumstances and worries have made them fragile from within. It keeps them constantly lost in the thought that if they fall behind in the affairs of life, they will immediately be excluded from their relationships by establishing their weakness as the basis. They don't even care about others.

Today, surviving each day of life is extremely challenging for everyone, especially after the Coronavirus pandemic, which has worsened the situation. This virus has left deep negative impacts on people from all walks of life, causing severe consequences wherever it has touched. It has caused a major economic crisis by devastating the economies, affecting individuals connected to every class and profession. Numerous people have lost their livelihoods, causing a decline in income, and even those in the high-income bracket have been directly affected by the virus. As a result, they had to make changes in their lifestyles due to the scarcity of resources. Remember that the complete eradication of the virus has not yet been achieved worldwide.

For God's sake, think and realize how people from various beliefs, races, and religions all over the world are facing difficult situations. They are enduring countless struggles, running in an endless race, and living a tiresome life. Every day becomes a significant test for each one of them. In this era of new times, it seems that new challenges and demands have multiplied infinitely. Those who are trying to fulfill them find themselves overwhelmed. Day and night, everyone is engulfed in these worries and anxieties.

How can we fulfill these responsibilities that have been assigned to us and those whose hopes are attached to us, whose eyes are watching our path? This very thought burdens the mind and increases restlessness and unease. Peace and contentment automatically vanish from our lives, and despair and sadness take control. This is why mental stress has become the greatest enemy of humanity in the present age, capturing almost the entire human race. The pain of losing tranquility and the desire to regain it inflict endless suffering upon everyone, which is evident on the faces of many people.

Now, the circle of mental tension is not limited to individuals with low income or status. It includes many famous and renowned personalities, high-ranking officials, and people burdened with immense wealth and power. Even those who lead lives of luxury and splendor, enjoying all the privileges, are not immune to its influence. This mental turmoil affects and continues to affect people from all walks of life, from the humblest to the most influential, from small households to grand mansions.

They are trapped in a web of confusion and are caught in the grips of mental disturbances in one way or another form.

Now, keeping this reality in mind, all the individuals who are part of our society and live among us must have faced similar situations at times. How do they cultivate hatred within themselves and burden themselves with it? How can anybody consider innocent people as their targets, who are already overwhelmed by their thousands of worries and thoughts and crushed under the weight of depression?

Time has made them restless. Peace has fled away from them, taking away the smiles from their faces. All kinds of comfort have become forbidden. Difficulties and hardships have surrounded them, creating a miserable state for them. Why not, understand the truth of human beings and awaken the sense of humanity within ourselves? The innocent people living in the world have no enmity with anyone, no involvement in any kind of disputes, and no fear of any kind. They just lead their lives by focusing on their work, busy day and night in the race for survival under the scorching sun or the cold. Only they know their true condition. People of all beliefs are included in this. In this self-centered world, today's generation is fighting every battle of life alone. They, with their courage, endure all kinds of sorrows and pains and also heal themselves. Because they know that by expressing their troubles to some other person, he or she will not show any compassion and instead will try to take advantage of his or her tears. That's why everyone silently tolerates all kinds of troubles and worries.

Therefore, present-day humanity needs compassion and empathy, not aggravating the situations everyone is already struggling with in different names. We should make an effort to understand the truth that we often ignore by turning our heads away from it. In reality, our Creator, Sustainer, and the one who brought us into existence are the same for everyone. He does not discriminate against anyone anywhere. He is the one who provides the air, the light of the sun, and the water without which human existence is impossible. By making them accessible to every creature, everyone can benefit from them. The entire universe is sustained by His system. No one can claim exclusive ownership over these resources. He does not show any favoritism in matters of sustenance. He even takes note of the smallest grain of food and ensures it reaches its intended recipient. This sometimes astonishes the human intellect.

And it gives to whomever it wishes without any accountability, without considering good or bad. For the birth of a human, a single principle and method has been established for everyone. The mother who gives birth to a child has the same color and the same taste of milk in her breasts. Any child, regardless of their forced circumstances, can drink from another belief. Death remains constant for everyone. Its charm is to touch everyone at their appointed time, no matter how great their power may be. It does not spare the highest position, rank, or authority. No one can save themselves from death. The creation of humans, from head to toe, follows the same order. By bringing people from different parts of the world into existence, the same shape and form were given to them, so that recognizing each other becomes easy for everyone. Even though people in the world have different features and appearances, the color of the running blood in their veins remains the same. So that a sense of unity is established in everyone, and the possibility of mutual animosity based on any form or type is eliminated.

Nature

Human nature refers to the fundamental characteristics, qualities, and behaviors that are inherent to human beings. It encompasses the common and underlying traits that are believed to be universally present in humans, regardless of cultural, social, or individual differences.

Wherever there is any calamity, the people living there, in one way or another, become victims of it, getting trapped in their aftermath. Their cries and the conditions they face immediately become a matter of concern for everyone, and many welfare organizations come forward to help them, without seeking any belief or considering differences of race or color. It is due to the same blood that runs in everyone's veins and the influence of the milk found in all mothers, which nourishes everyone. In such situations, when everyone gathers their blood to help those trapped in calamities, it creates a sense of restlessness and impatience to assist them, and anyone can save someone's life by giving their blood. It is not necessary to have some particular belief, race, or lineage, being a human is enough because there is no trace of any bias in the blood of any creature.

If this is not enough to open our eyes, then we should concentrate on the recent Coronavirus. It is the same virus that, in the blink of an eye, turned into a pandemic, engulfing the whole world. It changed the perception and halted the pace of the world. Due to the lockdown, everyone stood still, confined to their own homes. Even the mighty powers of the world, despite having all the resources and means, couldn't escape the clutches of this virus. They all stand helpless and in deep pain. A considerable number of people, regardless of their beliefs, have lost their lives in the face of this virus, leaving behind their dreams and aspirations, bidding farewell to the world. The world still hasn't completely overcome this scourge. Almost everyone, in some way or another, has been affected by the damages caused by this virus, whether they belong to any ideology, race, or religion. No matter how hard individuals tried, they couldn't protect themselves from the impact of this virus, from the lowest to the highest levels. If one's mind still doesn't open, it can lead to great misfortune. The Coronavirus didn't discriminate on color, race, or religion; no one can claim that their believers were spared by the virus, and none of our individuals were affected by it. Why wouldn't people realize it now? Those, who always burn in the fire of prejudice and arrogance, belittling others and claiming superiority, at the very least, the Coronavirus has taught us to eliminate this division. It taught us that it didn't target anyone based on personal beliefs or ideologies; it just saw everyone as human beings. It revealed that for me, everyone is equal. Now, if we dig into the depths of this Coronavirus, which has erected mountains of difficulties and afflictions upon people around the world, causing immense financial and human losses, it has shattered all records of grief and pain. In it, there is also significant advice for everyone, which can be understood if we make a genuine effort.

We belong to the same brotherhood and the same community. The practical proof of this is that the virus, by creating similar situations, has brought everyone together in the same line. It has affected everyone equally, causing them to face the same difficulties and troubles. Therefore, everyone, in one way or another, has experienced the reality of pain caused by this virus through practical observation.

So all those people who, through hatred, put innocent people in trouble and add to their hardships, have understood this through the Coronavirus. One who has experienced the pain knows what it feels like to turn someone's life upside down and create a miserable condition for him or her. And this happened simultaneously when most people in the world realized its impact. They witnessed its effects on themselves.

Therefore, this virus does teach a lesson to those people who, through any form of hateful thinking, turn innocent people into their enemies and, in various ways, contribute to their suffering and miseries. Isn't it enough for them to understand that they have to become victims of situations?

The pain caused by it is known only to the person who has experienced it. It disrupts an individual's life, turning it into a state of turmoil. And there is a truth that we are oblivious to, which our attention doesn't even touch. Good and compassionate human beings are slowly fading away from humanity. It is a self-perception of a human being that has already been proclaimed. In essence, humans have been bestowed with the rank of the noblest creation, meaning the highest and most superior among all creatures in the world we know. Now, try to understand the depth of this realization. This realization has not been acquired in the same way. It has been obtained through the qualities that distinguish it from others. It is the possession of superior intellect and consciousness, which enables it to think and understand. It teaches the ability to differentiate between right and wrong, good and evil, with ease. A special attribute has been given to its heart so that it always keeps in mind the respect and compassion for the worth of human beings in its eyes. Now, try to understand why a human being has been endowed with so much virtue. Now, make an effort to understand that by harboring any kind of hatred, we are depriving ourselves of all those virtues and qualities that set us apart from other creatures. So, if we truly comprehend and make an effort to understand what it means to be human, the question does not arise as to how hatred can arise between humans. We have limited ourselves to a certain personality and have never made an effort to find the essence of humanity within ourselves, which has been honored with a great title. So, its consequence is evident. Hatred has spread throughout the world, and its markets have been established in most places. And seeing how hatred is escalating around the world, it is felt that although the population of humans is increasing, the number of human beings is decreasing rapidly. The graph of humanity is falling day by day. The reason is that it has become a rogue and a rebel against its beliefs because every thought has been rigidly directed and instructed to embrace humanity and attach great importance to all its principles and regulations.

By acting against their own beliefs and tarnishing their reputation, people are causing significant harm. Every religion and every ideology has placed humanity at its core. When tested, an individual has the right to be called a follower of their beliefs. If they lack humanity, then they are not truly following their own beliefs. Even if such individuals spend days and nights reciting the beads of knowledge of their beliefs, they will not benefit from it. Instead, by doing so, they are going against the principles they have been taught and instructed to follow. Respecting and honoring human values and dignity in all circumstances is obligatory for everyone. Now, if someone, after understanding the fundamental teachings and principles of their beliefs, is not willing to acknowledge and understand the value and importance of humanity, they should understand that Satan (the devil) is leading them astray and deceiving them. And what this devil always desires is to perpetuate divisions and hatred in the world, to the extent that eradicating humanity from the world becomes easy and convenient. People will then naturally become instruments to eliminate it. By making humanity his or her own, he or she becomes a human, and by abandoning humanity, he or she becomes a beast.

We are witnessing numerous horrifying and heart-wrenching incidents across the world in the name of hatred. Many people have turned against their fellow human beings, treating them as enemies and preying on their lives and possessions like hungry wolves. They have turned their hearts into stones, cutting off the cords of compassion and fear in their souls, and have openly declared war against humanity. The fire of hatred within them has generated a frenzy, and innocent people have become their targets, and they are subjecting them to unimaginable suffering. These incidents are not hidden, and they challenge anyone who believes in humanity, causing deep wounds in their hearts. It raises the question of whether the human beings of the twenty-first century, despite claiming to be the era of enlightenment and consciousness, are using their intellect and capabilities. The reality before us shames humanity. Today, humanity, with all its compassion, is being replaced by hatred in an alarming manner, without any provocation or mistake, with innocent people being victimized and subjected to inhumane treatment, which signifies the decline of society itself. It seems that we have regressed to the Dark Ages, perhaps much before the Stone Age.

We are witnessing that a large number of people worldwide, who are associated with every belief, are giving their full support to the devil's tactics and agendas, and are providing complete cooperation for the success of his mission. They are actively promoting such hateful ideologies under different names, making innocent and blameless people their enemies. By targeting such people, they are deliberately undermining their confidence, making their daily lives a source of constant distress. They have made it their routine to criticize and humiliate these individuals through their actions, tarnishing the name of humanity and leaving no room for dignity and respect.

Deceptions

Deception refers to the act of intentionally misleading or tricking others through the use of false information, concealment of the truth, or manipulation of facts or perceptions. It involves deliberately presenting a distorted, inaccurate, or incomplete version of reality to gain an advantage, achieve a desired outcome, or deceive someone for personal gain.

People are living in such a big deception who, to associate hatred with humanity, are turning their backs on it. They are directly attacking their conscience, inflicting injustice upon themselves by committing atrocities in line with their beliefs. In reality, humanity itself grants the right to any human being to be called a true follower of their beliefs by making them complete and incorporating them into their principles. Embracing humanity and adhering to its principles is actually for their benefit and well-being.

Therefore, anyone who harbors any form of hatred, prejudice, or arrogance within themselves cannot reach their destination, because such a path passes only through humanity. Such individuals fail to comprehend the devilish scheme that turns them into enemies of humanity, utilizing their hearts and minds to fuel their hatred. As a result, they become deprived of all their human qualities and virtues, standing against humanity itself and becoming ready to forsake all the goodness and merits associated with it. Moreover, to misguide them further, a fabricated sense of satisfaction is induced within them, awakening a delusional state that undermines their genuine human traits and trust.

Spreading hatred under the disguise of belief is a harmful and destructive behavior. It involves using one's beliefs, often religious or ideological, as a pretext to promote or justify discriminatory attitudes, prejudice, or harmful actions toward others. It is important to recognize that beliefs themselves are not inherently negative, as they can provide individuals with guidance, purpose, and moral frameworks. However, when beliefs are misused or distorted to spread hatred, it becomes a serious problem.

Hatred and prejudice can take many forms, such as racism, religious intolerance, sexism, homophobia, xenophobia, and supremacism. Individuals who engage in spreading hatred often use their beliefs as a cover or justification for their discriminatory actions or views. They may use selective interpretations of religious texts, political ideologies, or cultural norms to reinforce their biases and target certain groups.

It is crucial to differentiate between the genuine expression of beliefs and the misuse of beliefs to justify harm. Freedom of belief and expression are important human rights, but they should not be used as a shield to spread hatred or incite violence. Society needs to promote open dialogue, critical thinking, and empathy to challenge and address hateful beliefs disguised as legitimate viewpoints.

It is also essential for individuals to be discerning and critical when encountering information or messages that promote hatred. Engaging in respectful conversations, questioning the motives behind certain beliefs, and seeking reliable sources of information can help combat the spread of hatred and discrimination.

Ultimately, fostering understanding, tolerance, and respect for diverse perspectives is the key to countering the spread of hatred disguised as belief. Education, awareness, and promoting inclusivity can contribute to building a more harmonious and accepting society.

Divisions

Divisions refer to the state of being divided or separated into distinct parts, groups, or categories. It implies a lack of unity or cohesion, where individuals or entities are separated or differentiated based on various factors, such as beliefs, ideologies, interests, and backgrounds.

Spreading hatred can indeed have destructive consequences and create divisions among people. It fosters animosity, fuels conflict, and undermines the principles of empathy and understanding that are essential for a harmonious society. When individuals engage in spreading hatred, they contribute to an environment of negativity and hostility, which can have far-reaching implications.

By sowing seeds of hatred, people not only harm the targets of their animosity but also damage the fabric of society as a whole. It erodes trust, cultivates prejudice, and perpetuates discrimination. Hatred can lead to discrimination, violence, and even acts of terrorism. It inhibits progress and hampers efforts toward unity, cooperation, and mutual respect.

Individuals need to realize the consequences of their actions and the potential harm they can cause by promoting hatred. Instead, we should strive for empathy, compassion, and understanding in our interactions with others. Promoting tolerance, acceptance, and respect for diversity can help foster a more inclusive and peaceful society.

While it is crucial to condemn and address instances of hatred, it is also important to engage in constructive dialogue, education, and efforts towards reconciliation. By fostering understanding and empathy, we can work towards breaking down barriers and building bridges between individuals and communities. Ultimately, promoting love, acceptance, and unity is essential for the well-being of humanity as a whole.

It's understandable to feel emotional and distressed when witnessing the negative impact that hatred, arrogance, and anti-human propaganda have on people's lives. These destructive behaviors can cause harm, division, and suffering within societies. It's natural to empathize with those affected and be saddened by the lack of empathy and compassion displayed by individuals who promote such attitudes.

Recognizing and reacting to the negative consequences of these behaviors is important for fostering a more inclusive and harmonious society. It's crucial to channel these emotions into positive actions that promote understanding, empathy, and respect among individuals. By supporting efforts to counteract hatred and promote kindness, we can contribute to a more compassionate and tolerant world.

The beginning of change

Remember that change starts with individuals and their choices. Advocating for empathy, educating others about the importance of inclusivity, and actively engaging in acts of kindness are ways to combat the negative effects of hatred and arrogance. Encouraging open dialogue, challenging discriminatory beliefs, and promoting human rights are also effective strategies to counteract anti-human propaganda.

While it's natural to feel emotional in the face of such negativity, it's important to maintain a sense of hope and focus on the potential for positive change. Each person can make a difference, and collective efforts can lead to a more compassionate and understanding society.

When people go against nature, they often face consequences and are often punished in various ways. Nature operates according to its own set of laws and principles, and when individuals or societies act in opposition to these natural processes, there can be negative repercussions.

In social and cultural contexts, going against nature can involve violating ethical principles and fundamental human rights. When people act in ways that oppress, exploit, or discriminate against others based on factors like race, gender, or social status, they create an imbalance in society. Such actions often lead to social unrest, conflicts, and a breakdown of trust, resulting in punishment in the form of social isolation, legal repercussions, or even revolutions.

Overall, going against nature disrupts the delicate balance that exists in the world and within human societies. While the punishment may not always be immediate or apparent, the consequences tend to manifest over time, affecting the well-being of individuals and societies. It is essential to respect and work in harmony with nature, as doing so promotes sustainability, health, and a more balanced and harmonious existence for all.

Remember that humanity should be a foremost belief, and harming fellow humans should not bring us happiness. Treating others with kindness, compassion, and respect is essential for fostering a harmonious and just society.

Humanity, in this context, refers to recognizing the inherent value and dignity of every human being, regardless of their background, beliefs, or circumstances. It means acknowledging that we are all part of the same global community and that our actions can have a significant impact on the well-being of others.

Harming fellow humans goes against the principles of empathy, fairness, and cooperation that are crucial for a thriving society. It can lead to suffering, injustice, and the erosion of trust between individuals and communities. In contrast, acts of kindness, understanding, and support can promote unity, happiness, and collective progress.

It is important to cultivate empathy and strive for peaceful resolutions to conflicts, rather than resorting to violence or cruelty. By treating others with respect and working together to address common challenges, we can build a more compassionate and harmonious world.

Ultimately, promoting the well-being of our fellow humans should be a guiding principle that informs our actions, decisions, and interactions with others.

Fundamentally, humanity serves as an air traffic controller to embrace every belief, thought, ideology, and religion. It becomes essential for every pilot to adhere to its system, maintaining constant communication during flights to ensure the safety and protection of passengers and crew, allowing the aircraft to reach its destination securely. However, if any aviator despite his experience and skills disobeys the regulations of air traffic control, neglects its significance disconnects from the system, and flies independently, is sure to endanger the lives of all the passengers.

Introspection

Let us introspect ourselves and realize that we are practicing the belief that emphasizes humanity. Instead of following our own belief of connection with humanity, we are disconnecting the two.

The increasing chaos, turmoil, corruption, bloodshed, and violent incidents around the world are because we have forgotten the lessons of humanity. We were supposed to follow the path guided by the humanity system. However, we have strayed from it, following our whims and desires. This very reason has allowed many people to exploit hatred for their benefit. By creating a justification to commit injustice and cruelty against them, many innocent people are subjected to ruthless treatment. There can be nothing worse than this flaw. We are Hindus, Muslims, Sikhs, Buddhists, Christians, Jews and much more. We are everything, but are we humans? This is the question we must ponder.

Blinded and deafened by intense hatred, come from every division and class. If only they would try once to know and understand the truth that whether the knife falls on the melon or the melon on the knife, it is always the melon that has to bear the brunt. Amid the hatred, innocent humans get caught, with everyone going against them and all kinds of accusations being thrown at them. The world continues to oppress them with injustice and excessive cruelty, making them helpless and marginalized. Unfortunately, it has now become a common practice, and more unfortunately people seem to accept it without giving it serious thought and consideration!

Although, the cries and screams of the oppressed are taken lightly, who knows how much power lies hidden in their sighs and tears, a power that can shake the entire universe. Because the sighs of the oppressed, regardless of their race, religion, or belief, break through all barriers and obstacles, and reach the Almighty to compel nature to take action. Then the Higher Power comes to their rescue by declaring the punishment and unleashes its wrath, which spares no one in any form or appearance. The punishment then makes everyone suffer, with no regard for anyone. In front of that great power, no means or instruments, no matter how mighty, can resist or save anyone.

While it is true that there are individuals who prioritize their interest's only and spread hatred and arrogance, it is important to acknowledge that there are also many people who genuinely care about the well-being and betterment of humanity as a whole. These individuals are motivated by compassion, empathy, and a desire to make a positive impact on the world.

People who care for humanity often engage in various acts of kindness, generosity, and service. They may volunteer their time and resources to help those in need, support charitable causes, advocate for human rights, work towards social and environmental justice, or contribute to scientific and technological advancements that benefit society. Their actions can range from small gestures of kindness in their local communities to larger-scale efforts that address global issues.

The presence of these individuals is crucial for the progress and development of society. Their dedication and commitment inspire others and create a ripple effect, encouraging more people to get involved and make a difference. They provide hope, solidarity, and a sense of unity, reminding us that positive change is possible.

Moreover, their actions can have far-reaching impacts, improving the lives of individuals, communities, and even future generations. They contribute to the advancement of knowledge, foster collaboration and cooperation, and promote values such as equality, justice, and compassion.

In essence, the presence of people who care for humanity is instrumental in shaping a better world. Their efforts remind us of our shared responsibility to each other and encourage us to strive for a more inclusive, empathetic, and sustainable future.

At the same time, it is unfortunate that there are individuals whose thinking and actions have resulted in harm and damage to the world. These individuals may be driven by greed, selfishness, or a disregard for the consequences of their actions on others.

Some individuals and corporations prioritize short-term profits over long-term sustainability, leading to practices that harm ecosystems, contribute to climate change, and deplete natural resources.

People who engage in warfare, violence, and hate, can cause immense suffering, destabilizing regions and impacting global security.

Individuals who perpetuate discrimination, exploitation, or systemic injustices contribute to social divisions, hinder progress, and deny basic rights and opportunities to marginalized communities.

Individuals involved in corrupt practices undermine institutions, erode trust, and divert resources meant for public welfare, resulting in economic damage and a lack of progress.

Some people intentionally spread false information, leading to confusion, polarization, and the undermining of public trust in institutions, including science and journalism.

These harmful actions can have widespread and long-lasting effects, impacting not only the present but also future generations. They hinder progress toward a more sustainable, just, and harmonious world.

Understandably, the majority of us may perceive a loss of peace and tranquility in the world, as some numerous ongoing challenges and conflicts overshadow moments of peace. However, it is important to note that peace and tranquility are complex concepts influenced by various factors, and the state of the world can be seen differently depending on one's perspective and the specific regions or issues being considered.

Acknowledgments

While it is true that conflicts, violence, hatred, and tensions exist in different parts of the world, it is essential to recognize that there are also regions and communities experiencing relative stability and peaceful coexistence.

It is crucial not to overlook the positive developments that have occurred globally. For example, advancements in technology and communication have brought people from different cultures and backgrounds closer together, fostering understanding and empathy. Many countries have made significant progress in terms of human rights, reducing poverty, and improving living standards. Additionally, international organizations and initiatives are working towards addressing global challenges such as climate change, and inequality, and promoting sustainable development.

While there are setbacks and ongoing struggles, it is important to acknowledge the individuals, organizations, and movements dedicated to promoting peace, justice, and harmony. By amplifying their efforts and supporting initiatives that promote dialogue, understanding, and cooperation, we can contribute to creating a more peaceful and tranquil world.

It is also essential for individuals to foster peace and tranquility within their immediate surroundings, by cultivating empathy, respect, and understanding in their interactions with others. Small acts of kindness and compassion can have a positive wave effect and contribute to a more peaceful and harmonious environment.

Prioritizing humanity over wealth can play a significant role in fostering peace and love in the world. While wealth and economic development are important for societal progress, true peace and tranquility are ultimately rooted in the values and actions that prioritize the well-being and dignity of all human beings.

When we prioritize humanity, we acknowledge the inherent worth and rights of every individual, regardless of their background, socio-economic status, or any other characteristic. This recognition promotes inclusivity, equality, love, and respect for diversity, which are essential foundations for peaceful coexistence.

There are many ways in which emphasizing humanity can contribute to a more peaceful world:

Recognizing and understanding the experiences, struggles, and aspirations of others cultivates empathy and compassion. By putting ourselves in others' shoes and treating them with kindness and empathy, we can foster understanding, build bridges, and reduce conflict.

Valuing humanity involves engaging in open, honest, and respectful dialogue. By actively listening to different perspectives and seeking common ground, we can find peaceful resolutions to conflicts, bridge divides, and build mutually beneficial relationships.

Prioritizing humanity entails addressing systemic injustices and striving for social equality. By promoting equal access to resources, opportunities, and rights, we can mitigate the underlying causes of conflict and create a more just and harmonious society.

Emphasizing humanity encourages collaboration, love, and cooperation across borders, cultures, and ideologies. By recognizing our shared humanity and interconnectedness, we can work together to address global challenges such as poverty, climate change, and conflicts, thereby promoting peace on a broader scale.

Prioritizing humanity involves educating ourselves and others about the value of peace, human rights, love, affection, and the importance of fostering a culture of empathy, understanding, and respect. By promoting education that nurtures critical thinking, empathy, and global citizenship, we can empower individuals to contribute to a more peaceful world.

When we place humanity at the center of our decisions, actions, and policies, we create a foundation that fosters peace, understanding, and harmony. By valuing and respecting the inherent worth and dignity of all individuals, we contribute to a more just, compassionate, and peaceful world.

Love

Love is a complex and multifaceted emotion that is deeply experienced and expressed by humans. It encompasses a range of positive and profound feelings, attitudes, and behaviors towards oneself, others, and even things or ideas. Love is often associated with affection, care, compassion, empathy, and a deep sense of connection.

Love has the potential to bring peace to the world, while hatred can contribute to creating a hostile and distressing environment. Love and hatred are powerful emotions that shape our interactions and relationships with others, ultimately influencing the state of the world we live in.

When love prevails, it fosters understanding, empathy, and compassion. Love allows us to forgive and seek reconciliation, even in the face of past conflicts or grievances. It opens the door for healing and moving forward, promoting peace between individuals and communities.

Love encourages respect for diversity and the acceptance of others as they are. When we approach others with love, we recognize their inherent worth and rights, fostering an inclusive and harmonious society.

Love inspires cooperation and collaboration, as it encourages us to work together towards shared goals. By recognizing our interconnectedness and supporting one another, we can address common challenges and promote peace on a larger scale.

Love enables us to empathize with others and understand their perspectives, even when they differ from our own. This empathy builds bridges of understanding, reduces prejudice, and fosters peaceful dialogue and resolution of conflicts.

On the other hand, hatred fuels division, conflict, and suffering. When hatred prevails, it can lead to violence and aggression. Hatred can drive individuals or groups to engage in violent acts, perpetuating cycles of harm and escalating conflicts.

Hatred often results in discrimination, prejudice, and the marginalization of certain individuals or communities. This can lead to social tensions and unrest.

Hatred can create deep divisions and animosity between different groups, contributing to a hostile and contentious societal atmosphere.

Hatred can be harnessed to promote destructive ideologies that dehumanize others and justify violence or oppression.

In summary, love has the potential to create a peaceful world by fostering forgiveness, respect, cooperation, and empathy. Conversely, hatred breeds conflict, division, and suffering. Choosing love over hatred in our thoughts, actions, and relationships is a powerful step toward creating a more peaceful and harmonious world.

Leadership

Those in positions of power, such as rulers and state administrative officers, indeed have a crucial responsibility to uphold and work on the principles of humanity. As leaders, they have the authority and influence to shape policies, make decisions, and set an example for others. Their actions and choices can significantly impact the well-being and rights of individuals and communities within their jurisdiction.

Leaders, (read ministers, administrative officers) have a moral duty to serve the best interests of their citizens and promote the common good. Embracing humanity means valuing the dignity, rights, and well-being of all individuals under their governance.

By promoting policies and practices that prioritize humanity, leaders contribute to social stability. This involves ensuring equal access to opportunities, justice, and necessities, which can help reduce social disparities and prevent grievances that can lead to conflicts.

Leaders who prioritize humanity and act in the best interests of their constituents build trust and legitimacy. When leaders demonstrate empathy, transparency, and accountability, they foster a sense of trust and cooperation between the government and the people it serves.

Leaders who work on the principles of humanity recognize the importance of sustainable development. They understand the need to balance economic growth with social and environmental considerations, ensuring that resources are utilized responsibly and equitably for the benefit of present and future generations.

Leaders have the power to inspire and influence others through their actions and values. By embodying the principles of humanity, they can inspire citizens, communities, and even other leaders to follow suit and prioritize the well-being and rights of all individuals.

Leaders need to adopt a human-centric approach in their decision-making processes, considering the impacts on vulnerable populations, promoting social justice, and addressing systemic inequalities. By doing so, they contribute to building a more inclusive, just, and compassionate society.

Although it is not solely the responsibility of leaders to work on the principles of humanity, however, leaders of all types, may they be politicians, government officials, or religious and community leader role is always pivotal in this regard. Such people also remain on the radar of the common masses, hence play as role models.

The role of leaders is indeed crucial in providing various forms of justice to the people they govern. Justice encompasses several dimensions, including social justice, economic justice, and legal justice, among others.

These leaders have the power to shape social policies and create an inclusive society that upholds fairness and equality. They can work towards eliminating discrimination, prejudice, and bias, and ensure that everyone has equal opportunities and access to resources, regardless of their race, gender, religion, or socioeconomic background.

They can implement policies that address income inequality, poverty, and wealth disparity. They can strive to create a fair economic system that provides opportunities for upward mobility and ensures a decent standard of living for all citizens.

Leaders are responsible for upholding the rule of law and ensuring that the legal system operates fairly and impartially. They can work towards creating an independent judiciary, strengthening law enforcement agencies, and promoting access to justice for all members of society. Leaders can also advocate for reforms that address systemic issues within the legal system, such as reducing racial disparities in sentencing and improving the effectiveness of the criminal justice system.

Leaders can promote restorative justice approaches that focus on healing, rehabilitation, and reconciliation instead of solely punitive measures. They can support initiatives that encourage dialogue, mediation, and community involvement to resolve conflicts and repair harm caused by criminal activities or social injustices.

On the contrary corrupt leadership leads to widespread injustice within a society. When leaders engage in corrupt practices, they prioritize their interests or the interests of a select few over the well-being and rights of the general population. This can result in various forms of injustice.

Corrupt and biased leadership often leads to economic inequality and unfair distribution of resources. Corrupt leaders may embezzle public funds, accept bribes, and engage in illicit financial activities, depriving society of essential resources that could be used for public welfare and development. As a result, basic services such as healthcare, education, and infrastructure suffer, exacerbating economic disparities.

Corrupt leaders engage in nepotism and favoritism, granting privileges and opportunities to their family members, friends, or associates. This leads to social inequality and undermines meritocracy. Marginalized groups and vulnerable populations face further discrimination and exclusion, perpetuating social injustice within society.

Such kind of leadership can manipulate the legal system, compromising the rule of law and undermining the administration of justice. They may interfere with judicial processes, manipulate verdicts, and protect individuals involved in corrupt activities. This erodes public trust in the legal system and creates a culture of impunity, where the powerful can escape accountability.

Hence, people at the helm or with leaders of any sort should indeed feel fortunate to be in a position of power and authority where they have the opportunity to make a positive impact on people's lives and provide better services. Leadership comes with the responsibility to serve and work for the well-being of the community and the individuals they represent. When leaders approach their role with a sense of gratitude and appreciation for the opportunity to create positive change, it can foster a mindset of empathy, responsibility, and dedication.

Feeling fortunate can help leaders stay connected to the needs and aspirations of the people they serve. It can drive them to actively seek out ways to improve services, address social issues, and uplift the quality of life for their constituents. By recognizing their privileged position, leaders can cultivate a sense of humility and a commitment to serving the greater good rather than pursuing personal gain or self-interest.

Furthermore, a sense of gratitude can also foster a collaborative and inclusive approach to leadership. When leaders acknowledge that they are part of a larger collective, they are more likely to engage with the diverse perspectives and needs of the community. This can lead to more participatory decision-making processes, where input from various stakeholders is valued, and policies are formulated with the input and consent of the people affected.

However, it is important to note that feeling fortunate should not be a justification for complacency or a lack of accountability. Leaders must use their position of privilege to actively address systemic issues, promote justice, and work toward the betterment of society. They should constantly strive to improve their leadership skills, remain responsive to the evolving needs of the people, and demonstrate a genuine commitment to serving the public interest.

Leadership should be driven by a sense of gratitude, purpose, and the desire to make a positive difference in people's lives, with a strong focus on providing better services and promoting the overall well-being of the community.

The spirit of service

And indeed, serving mankind brings immense pleasure and satisfaction to individuals in positions. When leaders dedicate themselves to the service of others, it can be a deeply fulfilling experience.

Serving others allows leaders to make a tangible impact on people's lives. Seeing positive changes, improvements, and transformations resulting from their efforts can provide a sense of purpose and meaning. Knowing that their actions have made a difference in the well-being and happiness of others can be incredibly rewarding.

Engaging in service requires leaders to develop empathy and connect with the needs, struggles, and aspirations of others. It helps them understand the challenges faced by different individuals and communities, creating a sense of connection and shared humanity. Building these connections and working together to address problems can foster a sense of fulfillment and satisfaction.

When leaders and those at the helm witness the positive impact of their service, they often receive gratitude and recognition from the people they have helped. This appreciation can be emotionally fulfilling, reinforcing the importance and value of their work. The recognition and appreciation from others can provide a sense of validation and satisfaction in knowing that their efforts are acknowledged and valued.

Engaging in service requires leaders to develop various skills, such as empathy, communication, problem-solving, and collaboration. Through the process of serving others, leaders often experience personal growth and development. Overcoming challenges, learning from diverse perspectives, and finding innovative solutions can contribute to a sense of satisfaction and fulfillment.

Many people with power are driven by a sense of higher ideals and a desire to contribute to the greater good. By serving mankind, they align their actions with their values and principles, which can bring a profound sense of fulfillment. Working towards creating a more just, equitable, and compassionate society can be deeply rewarding on a personal and moral level.

It is important to note that the pleasure and satisfaction derived from serving mankind should not be the sole motivation for leadership. It should be accompanied by a genuine commitment to the well-being and empowerment of others, and a willingness to address systemic issues and promote justice. True fulfillment comes from the positive impact made and the enduring legacy left behind, rather than seeking personal gratification alone.

But unfortunately, hatred, inhuman approach, and self-centeredness are contributing to the creation of numerous social problems in various societies. When individuals prioritize their interests or hold prejudiced views, it can lead to division, conflict, and the perpetuation of injustice.

Selfishness

Selfishness refers to a self-centered and excessive focus on one's interests, needs, desires, and well-being, often at the expense of others. It involves a lack of consideration or concern for the welfare and happiness of others and a tendency to prioritize personal gain or satisfaction over the needs of others.

Selfishness typically manifests as a disregard for the feelings, rights, or boundaries of others, and a willingness to manipulate or exploit situations to serve one's interests. It may involve actions that benefit one's self while disregarding the negative impact on others or failing to contribute to the well-being of others.

Hatred, arrogance, selfishness, and an inhuman approach can fuel discrimination and prejudice based on factors such as race, religion, gender, sexual orientation, or socioeconomic status. This has resulted in unequal treatment, marginalization, and the denial of rights and opportunities to certain groups. Discrimination and prejudice undermine social cohesion, hinder collective progress, and perpetuate systemic injustices.

Self-centeredness and an unwillingness to understand or empathize with others contribute to social polarization. When individuals only prioritize their interests and refuse to engage in dialogue or find common ground, it leads to the fragmentation of communities, the erosion of trust, and the breakdown of social bonds. This hinders cooperation, problem-solving, and the development of inclusive and harmonious societies.

Hatred and inhuman approach have escalated into violence and conflict. When individuals or groups harbor deep-seated animosity towards each other, it leads to aggression, hostility, and even acts of violence. These social problems not only cause immediate harm but also have long-lasting negative consequences, including the displacement of communities, loss of life, and psychological trauma.

Self-centeredness and a lack of concern for the well-being of others have perpetuated inequality and social injustice. When individuals prioritize their wealth and privilege over the needs of the broader society, it leads to the concentration of resources and power in the hands of a few, while leaving others in poverty and disadvantage. This exacerbates social divisions, hinders social mobility, and undermines the principles of fairness and equality.

Things to do

Addressing social problems requires a collective effort to foster empathy, understanding, and a sense of shared humanity. It involves promoting values such as compassion, respect, and social responsibility. Education, awareness campaigns, and promoting dialogue and understanding among diverse groups can contribute to the reduction of hatred, an inhuman approach, and self-centeredness, paving the way for a more inclusive and just society.

Leaders, in particular, play a critical role in addressing these social problems. They can set an example by promoting values of empathy, inclusivity, and social justice in their actions and policies. By fostering a culture of respect and understanding, leaders can contribute to the resolution of conflicts, the reduction of discrimination, and the promotion of a more compassionate and cohesive society.

Every conscious mind is rightly concerned about conflicts and the potential harm caused by people pursuing their interests. Promoting humanity and fostering a peaceful coexistence is indeed essential for a harmonious society. While human ideology and values play a crucial role in shaping our behavior, it is important to note that achieving lasting peace involves a multi-faceted approach.

Encouraging empathy and understanding between individuals and communities helps bridge divides. By recognizing and valuing the experiences, perspectives, and emotions of others, we can foster a sense of unity and reduce the likelihood of conflicts.

Open and respectful dialogue is vital for resolving conflicts and reaching common ground. Constructive conversations can promote understanding, generate innovative solutions, and help prevent tensions from escalating.

Educating people about the principles of peace, tolerance, and respect for diversity is crucial. By promoting education that instills critical thinking, empathy, and ethical values, we can create a more compassionate and informed society.

Establishing robust institutions, upholding the rule of law, and promoting accountable governance contribute to stability and peaceful coexistence. A just and fair legal framework ensures that conflicts can be addressed through peaceful means, offering a sense of security to all members of society.

Encouraging collaboration and cooperation at local, national, and international levels can lead to mutual benefits and shared prosperity. By fostering relationships based on trust and shared interests, we can overcome differences and work towards common goals.

While humanity and human ideology are essential, it is important to acknowledge that achieving peace is an ongoing and complex process. It requires collective efforts and a commitment to upholding the values of empathy, respect, and justice.

Time is indeed a valuable resource, and it is crucial to work towards the common good promptly to prevent further harm to humanity.

Efforts to promote peace should be pursued actively and with a sense of urgency. Individuals, communities, organizations, and governments need to prioritize peaceful means, over violence, and work towards sustainable solutions.

Global challenges require global solutions. Strengthening international cooperation and collaboration is crucial for addressing conflicts that transcend national boundaries. This includes supporting peacekeeping operations, promoting diplomatic initiatives, and upholding international human rights standards.

In a world that faces numerous challenges and conflicts, it is indeed crucial to reject hate and selfishness in favor of compassion, empathy, and selflessness.

Hate divides people and creates animosity. By embracing love, compassion, and understanding, we can foster a sense of unity and work together towards common goals.

Selfishness often leads to conflicts and violence. Choosing to prioritize peace and cooperation over personal interests can create an environment where people can coexist harmoniously and resolve differences through dialogue and understanding.

Hate and selfishness erode trust and damage relationships. Choosing kindness, empathy, and selflessness can nurture healthier and more meaningful connections with others, leading to stronger communities and bonds.

When we prioritize the well-being and needs of others alongside our own, we create an environment conducive to progress. Collaboration and cooperation based on shared values can lead to innovative solutions and collective advancement.

Shunning hate and selfishness can also have a positive impact on our personal growth and well-being. By embracing love, kindness, and empathy, we develop a greater sense of fulfillment, purpose, and happiness in our own lives.

Hate, selfishness, and the consequences they bring can indeed lead to suffering for individuals and communities. However, it is important to remember that suffering is not an inherent and inevitable outcome for humanity as a whole. Throughout history, human beings have shown resilience, adaptability, and the capacity to learn from past mistakes.

By recognizing the destructive nature of hate and selfishness, we can actively work towards minimizing their impact and promoting positive change. This requires collective efforts to foster empathy, understanding, and cooperation.

The advancements and knowledge gained by humanity have allowed us to uncover the secrets of nature and harness its power for our benefit. Now, we must recognize the significance of safeguarding ethical values to foster a world where love, understanding, and compassion prevail over harm and division.

Promoting ethical education can help instill values such as empathy, respect, and responsibility. By equipping individuals with the tools to navigate ethical dilemmas, we can encourage thoughtful decision-making and promote a culture of compassion.

Leaders in various fields, including politics, business, religion, and education, play a vital role in shaping ethical standards. Encouraging and supporting ethical leadership that prioritizes the well-being of others can have a profound impact on promoting a more compassionate and loving society.

Nurturing empathy and compassion is essential for fostering an environment where people embrace love instead of harm. Encouraging acts of kindness, promoting understanding of diverse perspectives, and practicing empathy towards others can help create a more inclusive and harmonious society.

Encouraging individuals to consider the ethical implications of their actions can contribute to a more conscientious society. Promoting critical thinking, and ethical reasoning, and encouraging dialogue about ethical dilemmas can help individuals make choices that prioritize love and well-being over harm.

While the journey towards safeguarding ethical values and promoting love over hatred may present challenges, it is an essential path to pursue for the betterment of humanity. By prioritizing ethical considerations, we can foster a world where people embrace each other in love, understanding, and mutual respect.

It is indeed disheartening to witness the presence of hatred in our world. It is of course frustrating and saddening to see individuals or groups who continue to spread hatred and division.

However, it is important to remember that change takes time, and progress towards a more loving and inclusive society is a collective effort. While some may still propagate hatred, it is crucial to focus on the positive actions and voices that are actively working to counteract hatred and promote love.

It is important to approach those who spread hatred with empathy and compassion. While their actions may be misguided or fueled by various factors, recognizing their humanity and engaging in respectful dialogue may open the door for understanding and change.

Be positive

Being positive refers to adopting a mindset and attitude that focuses on optimism, hope, and constructive thinking. It involves consciously choosing to see the brighter side of situations, approaching challenges with a proactive mindset, and cultivating a positive outlook on life and others.

Be a positive force by embodying the values you wish to see in the world. Spread love, tolerance, and respect in your interactions and relationships. By leading through actions and promoting a culture of empathy, we can inspire others to do the same.

Engage in meaningful conversations with others to promote understanding and bridge gaps. Seek common ground, listen actively, and share your perspectives respectfully. Such dialogues can challenge preconceived notions and foster empathy.

Embrace and celebrate diversity in all its forms. Encourage inclusivity and create spaces where different voices are heard and valued. By championing diversity, we can counteract the divisive ideologies propagated by those spreading hatred.

Remember, change takes time, but each effort can make a difference. By persistently promoting love, understanding, and unity, we can create a collective movement that inspires positive change and helps counteract the spread of hatred in our world.

Nourishing a compassionate and empathetic heart is crucial in fostering love, understanding, and positive interactions with others. When we cultivate a soft and open heart, we become more capable of experiencing and expressing empathy, kindness, and forgiveness.

Take time for self-reflection and introspection. Understand your own emotions, thoughts, and actions, and explore ways to cultivate compassion within yourself. This self-awareness lays the foundation for developing a softer heart towards others.

Empathy is the ability to understand and share the feelings of others. Practice putting yourself in someone else's shoes, seeking to understand their experiences and emotions. Engage in active listening and validate the feelings and experiences of others.

Small acts of kindness can have a significant impact. Practice acts of kindness towards others, whether through simple gestures, volunteering, or helping those in need.

These acts not only benefit others but also nurture a compassionate heart within yourself.

Letting go of grudges and practicing forgiveness allows us to free ourselves from negative emotions. Cultivate forgiveness towards those who have wronged you, recognizing the shared humanity and the potential for growth and healing.

Foster respectful and compassionate communication in your interactions with others. Choose words and tones that promote understanding, avoid judgment, and listen actively. This creates an environment conducive to empathy and connection.

Instead of focusing on differences, seek common ground with others. Look for shared values and experiences that can build bridges and foster understanding. Embrace diversity and celebrate the richness it brings to our lives.

Remember that nourishing a soft heart is a continuous journey. It requires conscious effort, self-compassion, and patience. By cultivating a soft heart within yourself, you not only contribute to your well-being but also inspire others to embrace love, empathy, and compassion.

It is disheartening to hear that the victimization of innocent people appears to be on the rise. Such circumstances underscore the importance of addressing this issue and working towards a more just and secure society.

Raising awareness about different forms of victimization and educating people about their rights and available resources is crucial. By providing information and knowledge, individuals can better protect themselves and support those who have been victimized.

Building strong and resilient communities can help prevent victimization. Community engagement, creating safe spaces, and fostering a sense of belonging can promote solidarity and support networks, reducing the vulnerability of innocent individuals.

Those who engage in harmful actions and suppress their conscience are ultimately causing harm to themselves as well. When individuals ignore their moral compass and act in ways that go against their values, it can have detrimental effects on their emotional well-being, sense of integrity, and overall inner peace.

Engaging in harmful actions can lead to feelings of guilt, remorse, and shame. Ignoring one's conscience and acting in ways that harm others can create a heavy emotional burden that weighs on the individual's psyche.

When someone intentionally harms others, it erodes their self-worth and self-esteem. Acting against one's moral compass can create a sense of internal conflict and self-condemnation, leading to a diminished sense of self-value.

Harming others can strain relationships and lead to isolation. Trust is eroded, and meaningful connections may be severed, resulting in a sense of loneliness and disconnection from others.

Engaging in harmful actions leads to a damaged reputation and loss of trust from others. This can have long-lasting consequences on personal relationships, limiting opportunities for growth and success.

Suppressing one's conscience and engaging in harmful and hateful actions can create inner turmoil and conflict. The individual may struggle with internal moral dilemmas, leading to inner unrest and dissatisfaction.

Continuously engaging in hateful and harmful behaviors erodes one's capacity for empathy and compassion. Over time, individuals may become desensitized to the suffering of others, leading to a diminished ability to connect with and understand the emotions and experiences of others.

While it is true that the well-being of humanity and the well-being of nature are interconnected, human actions have a significant impact on the natural world, and it is crucial to strive for a harmonious and sustainable relationship with nature.

Our creator, the highest power can be happy with us only when we make his creatures happy and remain in harmony with them.

So don't let hatred dominate you. Hatred is a destructive force that can poison our minds, harm relationships, and perpetuate a cycle of negativity. Choosing to reject hatred and embracing love, understanding, and compassion can lead to personal growth, healthier relationships, and a more harmonious society.

Hatred consumes our emotional well-being, leading to anger, resentment, and stress. By letting go of hatred and cultivating positive emotions, such as love and forgiveness, we can experience greater inner peace and happiness.

Hatred perpetuates cycles of animosity and discrimination, leading to societal division. By embracing love and compassion, we contribute to a more harmonious and inclusive society where diverse perspectives are valued and respected.

Hatred hinders progress and cooperation. By letting go of hatred, we can foster collaboration, empathy, and shared goals, leading to collective advancements and a better future for all.

When hatred spreads, it can indeed have detrimental effects on the value and well-being of humanity as a whole. Hatred fosters division, animosity, and a lack of empathy, leading to a breakdown in relationships, trust, and cooperation.

Hatred undermines our capacity for compassion and understanding. It blinds us to the suffering of others and hampers our ability to empathize with different perspectives and experiences. Compassion is a fundamental aspect of our humanity, and its erosion diminishes our collective value.

Hatred fuels division and fosters an "us versus them" mentality. It hampers our ability to come together as a united human family to address common challenges and work towards shared goals. Unity is crucial for collective progress and the well-being of humanity.

Hatred often leads to the dehumanization of certain groups or individuals. It fuels discrimination, prejudice, and bigotry, which not only harms those who are targeted but also devalues the inherent worth and dignity of every human being.

Hatred hinders social progress. It obstructs the exchange of ideas, stifles creativity, and limits our ability to find inclusive and sustainable solutions to complex problems.

It is crucial to actively counteract the spread of hatred by promoting love, understanding, and empathy. Embracing our shared humanity, valuing diversity, and fostering a culture of compassion and respect are essential to preserving the value and dignity of humanity. Each individual has the power to make a difference through their actions, choices, and commitment to building a more inclusive and compassionate world.

Conclusion

Humanity is the basic belief and its progress is the real progress. It reflects a perspective that places a strong emphasis on the value and advancement of the human species as a whole. It suggests that the well-being and development of humanity should be the central focus and measure of progress.

The term "humanity" in this context can refer to the collective existence, potential, and qualities of human beings. It encompasses various aspects, such as our intellectual, social, cultural, and moral dimensions. The belief that humanity is fundamental implies that our common humanity should be respected, nurtured, and prioritized in all endeavors.

The notion that the progress of humanity is real progress suggests that progress should not be solely measured by material or technological gains, but rather by how they positively impact the lives of individuals and society as a whole.

This perspective often highlights the importance of promoting equality, justice, compassion, and sustainability. It emphasizes the need to address and overcome societal challenges, such as poverty, discrimination, and conflict to foster the progress and betterment of humanity.

The belief that humanity should remain in all situations come what may. It is this ideology that binds human beings together and prompts them to share in each other's pain and suffering and it is through this ideology, people can be protected from each other's evil.

We all need to understand the reality that the secret to learning lies in embracing the principles of humanity. No one can find peace by going against the fundamental principles of humanity. It is a fundamental truth that one who causes distress to others cannot find peace or comfort for him or herself, no matter how great his or her authority or power may be. One shows mercy to others and also receives kindness and compassion from the heavens in return.

While living in this world, everyone works in some way to earn his or her livelihood. Some hold high and prestigious governmental or non-governmental positions, while others engage in smaller tasks. The goal for everyone is the same: to fulfill their necessities. While pursuing their individual activities, everyone should keep in mind that the highest principles of humanity should not be overlooked.

Conclusion

Everyone receives compensation for his or her work, ensuring that his or her basic needs are met. However, if one performs his or her tasks while considering the fate of humanity, he or she receives compensation that leads to eternal happiness. Those who exploit the principles of humanity seemingly cause trouble for others but later face the consequences themselves.

It is essential to understand that no one owns the world after coming into it. Everyone will spend a few years here and eventually depart, the only point on which the entire world agrees. It would be wonderful if we all supported each other, held each other's hands, and became friends. So that when our turn comes to leave this world, we do not bear the burden of causing trouble to others, and everyone mourns our departure.

This wealth, power, prestige, responsibilities, and even poverty, destitution, helplessness, and compulsion will all remain here. We will leave here empty-handed. If someone benefits from someone else's work, it is because that person is meant to benefit. Let us accept this reality and begin living our lives accordingly.

END

www.ingramcontent.com/pod-product-compliance
Lightning Source LLC
LaVergne TN
LVHW041624070526
838199LV00052B/3232